SEP 30 2020

D0764428

WITHDRAWN

50 ANIMALS THAT HAVE BEEN TO SPACE

Jennifer Read
and
John A. Read

Formac Publishing Company Limited
Halifax

Text Copyright © 2020 Jennifer Read and John A. Read

All rights reserved. No part of this book may be reproduced or transmitted in any form or by any means, electronic or mechanical, including photocopying, or by any information storage or retrieval system, without permission in writing from the publisher.

Formac Publishing Company Limited recognize the support of the Province of Nova Scotia through the Department of Communities, Culture and Heritage. We are pleased to work in partnership with the Province of Nova Scotia to develop and promote our cultural resources for all Nova Scotians. We acknowledge the support of the Canada Council for the Arts, which last year invested $153 million to bring the arts to Canadians throughout the country. This project has been made possible in part by the Government of Canada.

Library and Archives Canada Cataloguing in Publication

Title: 50 animals that have been to space / Jennifer Read & John A. Read.
Other titles: Fifty animals that have been to space
Names: Read, Jennifer, 1984- author. | Read, John A., author.
Identifiers: Canadiana 20190173122 | ISBN 9781459506022 (hardcover)
Subjects: LCSH: Animal space flight—History—Juvenile literature. | LCSH: Manned space
    flight—Juvenile literature. | LCSH: Animal experimentation—Juvenile literature.
Classification: LCC TL793 .R43 2020 | DDC 629.45—dc23

Published by:
Formac Publishing
Company Limited
5502 Atlantic Street
Halifax, NS, Canada
B3H 1G4
www.formac.ca

Distributed in
Canada by:
Formac Lorimer Books
5502 Atlantic Street
Halifax, NS, Canada
B3H 1G4

Distributed in the US by:
Lerner Publisher Services
1251 Washington Ave. N.
Minneapolis, MN, USA
55401
www.lernerbooks.com

Printed and bound in Korea.
Manufactured by We Sp. Co., Ltd
Job #191002

TABLE OF CONTENTS

Introduction

Throughout the history of aerial and space flight, scientists have wanted answers to some basic questions about flying: Could people survive high in the sky? Would they be able to breathe while travelling at speed? Could living creatures survive in space — beyond Earth's atmosphere? They were not willing to risk a human life to find out. For this reason, in the history of flight, animals were almost always the first to fly.

The history of animals in space can be traced to the Cold War and the Space Race. The difficult experiments, particularly where the animals did not come back, were conducted by the Soviet Union and the United States. These two countries were racing to get the first soldiers into space. From a military standpoint, space is the ultimate "high ground," and at the time it was thought that winning in space would mean winning on the ground.

Industrialized countries spend billions of dollars on research to stay ahead in the Space Age, and unfortunately animals have often played an important and sacrificial part in advancing this agenda. It is difficult to ignore the fact that many of the experiments included in this book would be considered inappropriate by today's standards.

Scientific Paper available online.

Read the actual research paper! If you see this symbol it means that you can easily find the research online. It will be listed under **Research Papers** at the back of the book.

▶ This symbol indicates that videos about the experiment can be found on YouTube.

In the 1950s, animals often rode in V-2 rockets taken from the defeated German army.

Animals at Work Today

Animals continue to play an important role in science. High-school students still dissect frogs and pigs, and at universities, biology and medical science students often work with monkeys. These students use the skills they learn from these **dissections** when they grow up to be vets, doctors, and biologists.

The animals in this book won't be the last animals in space. Animals help scientists understand how humans will survive in space both in terms of the physical and psychological challenges. This knowledge has applications on Earth, in medical research, and many other fields.

Within one or two hundred years, humans may even move out into the solar system to live permanently. Homes could be built in giant space stations that rotate to create their own gravity. Or perhaps humans will live on Mars within giant air-filled domes. In the future, people could even live on a moon of Jupiter, such as Callisto, where **radiation** exposure would be lowest. And maybe they will take their pets, too.

CHAPTER 1
Preparing for Space

First Flight in a Man-Made Vehicle

On September 19, 1783, at Versailles, France, a rooster, a duck, and a sheep were placed in a basket attached to a hot-air balloon. With a large crowd cheering them on, Joseph-Michel and Jacques-Étienne Montgolfier filled their balloon with hot air causing it to lift into the sky. The balloon, called *Set Le Martial*, had no heat source of its own, so as the air cooled it descended. The flight lasted about eight minutes and the animals landed safely.

Why the birds?

The sheep was chosen to represent a human, the duck because it is used to flight, and the rooster because it is a non-flighted bird.

Montgolfier Brothers

Date: September 19, 1783
Species: Rooster, duck, and sheep
Objective: Prove hot-air balloon flight
Launch Vehicle: *Set Le Martial* Montgolfier Balloon
Maximum Altitude: 457.2 m (1,500 ft)

First Animals to Ride a Rocket

Two chickens named Adam and Eve became the first animals to fly in a rocket. They arrived safely at their destination and were then donated to the Calcutta Zoo, India. Inventor Stephen Smith had modified the rocket to provide **ventilation**, **stabilization**, and shock absorption. There was no parachute, a soft riverbank was used for landing the rocket. A snake named Miss Creepy rode a separate rocket. Her only companion was an apple. Both the snake and the apple arrived safely.

Stephen Smith (1891–1951), a dentist, policeman, and customs official, believed that rockets were the best method for delivering mail.

Rocket Delivery

Date: June 29, 1935
Species: Chicken and snake
Objective: Rocket power
Launch Vehicle: Rocket made by the Oriental Fireworks Company
Distance: 1 km (3,281 ft)
Principal Investigator: Stephen Smith

Rocket mail

Stephen Smith launched the first ever mail rocket on September 30, 1934. The rocket he used was made by a local fireworks company. Smith also used a rocket to send relief to an area that had been devastated by an earthquake.

III High Altitude Balloons

Cosmic radiation was one of the many concerns about sending a person into space. Once again animals went first. Black mice were often used because it was discovered that cosmic particles would turn their black hairs white. These flights also aided the development of life-support systems.

US Air Force: Project Manhigh

Date: 1950s
Species: Rats, mice, dogs, cats, monkeys, rabbits
Objective: Study cosmic radiation and controlled artificial environments
Launch Vehicle: Moby Dick and Manhigh balloons
Maximum Altitude: 90,000 ft
Principal Investigator: US Air Force and Dr. David Simons

Radiation

Electromagnetic radiation is light at different wavelengths, i.e., microwaves, radio waves, x-rays, ultraviolet, etc. When we talk about radiation in space, we're often talking about atomic nuclei either trapped in Earth's magnetic field or moving quickly as a cosmic ray.

High altitude balloon.

Black mouse with white hairs due to exposure to cosmic rays.

Dr. David Simons, army officer and physician, didn't just send animals up in high altitude balloons. He went up, too. He set an altitude record in 1957, soaring to more than 31 km (19 mi) above Earth attached to a helium balloon.

CHAPTER 2
Early Spaceflights

01 USAF: Project Albert

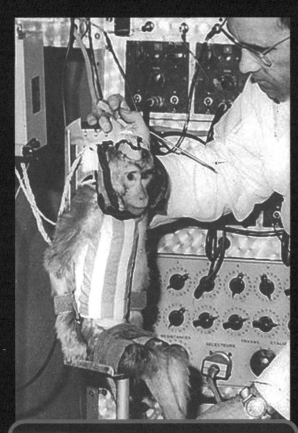

Albert the rhesus macaque was the first primate to ride a rocket. His launch vehicle was a V-2 rocket taken from the defeated German army after World War II. Before his flight, Albert was **anesthetized** so that he would not suffer if something went wrong during the flight. Sadly, the capsule parachute failed to open, and the spacecraft crashed.

On June 14, 1949, a second monkey, Albert II, became the first primate to reach space. Albert II reached an altitude of 137 km (85 mi). On the return, the parachute opened and began to slow the space capsule but soon after it failed and the capsule crashed.

Project Albert continued to suffer parachute failures resulting in the loss of several more monkeys (and a mouse). It was a small blessing that none of them were conscious when their rockets crashed.

USAF: Project Albert

Date: June 11, 1948–December 8, 1949
Species: Rhesus macaque monkeys
Objective: To return from space-flight
Launch Vehicle: V-2 rocket
Maximum Altitude: 137 km (85 mi)

Where does space begin?

The line that divides Earth's atmosphere from space is called the **Karman Line**. It was named after scientist Theodore von Karman and is defined internationally as 100 km (62.1 mi) above sea level.

02 First Dogs in Space

While the US was using monkeys for their test flights, the USSR turned to man's best friend. Their canine cosmonauts were taken from the streets of Moscow because mutts tend to be hardy. The Durov Animal Theatre, which had been teaching animals to perform amazing feats since 1912, was chosen to train the street dogs. Their founder, Vladimir Durov, preferred to use rewards instead of punishment to train animals. This was revolutionary at the time.

Soviet researchers used two dogs — Tsygan and Dezik — so that their reactions and vital signs could be compared during the space-flight. The rocket and parachute performed as designed and the first space dogs returned safely to Earth.

Tsygan and Dezik

Date: July 22, 1951
Species: Dog
Objective: Test rocket, capsule, and recovery; Monitor reactions to rocket flight
Launch Vehicle: R1-V rocket
Maximum Altitude: 100 km (62.1 mi)

Tsygan and Dezik were the first dogs in space.

Vladimir Durov was a circus trainer who used rewards instead of punishment.

03 Aerobee Animals

The American missions between 1948 and 1952 were conducted by the US Air Force. NASA was founded six years later.

Two monkeys, named Patricia and Michael, were given face masks and oxygen to keep them alive while they rode a rocket into space. Patricia was in an upright position while Michael was lying back. Scientists wanted to test which position was best for take-off and re-entry.

The Aerobee rocket, in which the animals travelled, is what is known as a **sounding rocket**. These rockets were specially designed for research.

Aerobee rocket.

Mildred and Albert, two mice, were included on the rocket flight as part of a study on weightlessness. One was given a perch to stand on and the other was not. All four animals on this short flight made it back safely.

USAF: Aerobee Animals

Date: May 21, 1952
Species: Philippine macaque monkeys and mice
Objective: Testing launch and re-entry positions and weightlessness
Launch Vehicle: Aerobee rocket
Maximum Altitude: 58 km (36 mi)

Mixed response

Not everyone agreed with putting animals in rockets. Some people even offered themselves as test subjects on future research flights.

04 Laika: First to Orbit Earth

Laika is perhaps the most famous animal to have been to space. She was the first animal to orbit the Earth. Laika was one of a group of ten dogs trained for this very important flight. The dogs were trained in simulation capsules where they were tested under different pressure, temperature, and oxygen conditions. Then they were trained to wear a waste removal apparatus (to keep the capsule poop free). Special space food was developed for the dogs that would contain both their food and water requirements in one jello-like substance. After an extensive review of all the dogs' test results (both physical and temperamental), Kudryavka — later known as Laika (barker) — was chosen. She was two years old and weighed 5 kg (11 lb).

Orbit vs suborbit

If you were to launch a rocket straight up, even hundreds of kilometres into space, the spacecraft would fall right back to Earth! That's because the spacecraft had not reached **orbit**. In addition to leaving the Earth's atmosphere, a rocket must also travel at 28,000 kph in a path that arcs around the Earth. Only then is the spacecraft in orbit. Any slower, and we call the flight **suborbital.**

Laika's flight was the first time that health data was sent from space by **telemetry**. Researchers recorded her heart-rate, blood pressure, movement, and breathing during the flight.

Laika

Date: October 27, 1957
Species: Dog
Objective: Achieve Earth orbit
Launch Vehicle: Sputnik 2 on an R-7 rocket
Destination: Low Earth orbit
Duration: 7 days

Viking Warrior's Funeral

On October 27, 1957, Laika was introduced to the public by radio broadcast. She obligingly barked her "hello."

The launch of the rocket was rushed to coincide with the anniversary of the Russian Revolution. Three days prior to launch, Laika was groomed, fitted with sensors, dressed in her spacesuit, and fastened into her capsule. During the three days Laika waited for her launch, scientists were able to check her vitals both manually and via telemetry to ensure that they were getting accurate readings. The equipment was also tested to ensure that everything was functioning as it should.

Finally, on November 3, 1957, Laika lifted off in her R-7 rocket. Telemetry showed that weightlessness had no ill effects on Laika and that her capsule held up as it should. Once she reached orbit, even her breathing and heart-rate returned to normal.

Unfortunately, some of the rocket's thermal insulation had been damaged during take-off and the cooling systems did not work as planned. Around 5 to 7 hours after becoming the first living thing to achieve Earth orbit, Laika succumbed to the extreme temperatures.

News of Laika's death was not released by Russia and when the world learned of the success of the launch, most people wanted to know if Laika would be rescued. Despite Laika's demise, data continued to be transmitted until November 10. On April 14, 1958, Sputnik 2 lost orbit and burned up on re-entry. Laika was given a Viking warrior's funeral. Her flight proved the viability of manned space-flight.

Memorials

In November 1997, a statue for fallen cosmonauts, including Laika, was unveiled at the Institute of Biomedical Problems in Star City, Moscow. On March 9, 2005, a patch of the Vostok crater on Mars was named Laika.

05 Project Mouse-In-Able (MIA)

USAF: Project MIA

Date: April 23 (Minnie), July 9 (Laska),
July 23 (Wickie), 1958
Species: Mice
Objective: Gauge reactions to space flight conditions
Launch Vehicle: Thor-Able Intermediate Range Ballistic Missile
Principal Investigator: US Air Force

Project Mouse-In-Able consisted of three rocket launches in 1958. This mission involved three mice and three separate rockets, all of which were lost and never found. The letters MIA stand for Mouse-In-Able (Able is the name of the rocket), but MIA is also an apt military term for "missing in action."

The first rocket carried a mouse named Minnie, but something went terribly wrong, and her rocket exploded.

A second rocket carried a mouse named Laska. Air Force scientists monitored her heart-rate during the flight and discovered that although her heart-rate increased with acceleration, it returned to normal once the mouse became weightless in space. The tiny spacecraft re-entered Earth's atmosphere, but unfortunately researchers were unable to locate it.

The third flight carried a mouse named Wickie. Like Laska's spacecraft, researchers were unable to find it once it had landed.

Rations

Wickie (shown in picture) was provided with 6 weeks worth of food, water, and oxygen.

Mice in the USAF

The United States Air Force (USAF) used small sounding rockets to test all sorts of things in space. Despite the fact that the Soviet Union had launched dogs into space, American researchers had yet to prove for themselves that animals could survive the journey.

Thor-Able rocket.

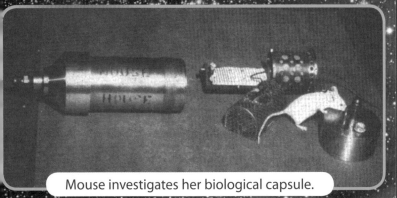

Mouse investigates her biological capsule.

Rocket stages

It takes a lot of energy to carry fuel tanks and rocket engines. This is why rockets often have multiple "stages." Each stage contains rocket engines and rocket fuel. Once a stage runs out of fuel, it falls away, and the remaining spacecraft ignites a second rocket (on the second stage) and continues toward space. Thor was the first stage of the rocket, and Able was the second.

06 Army Monkeys Able and Baker

Able strapped into her custom couch.

Two Monkeys, named Able and Baker, by order of the United States Army, were trained by the US Navy for a 1959 mission. They, and 26 other monkeys, completed many tests and space-simulations, and only the best-trained monkeys got to fly into space. On board the same Jupiter rocket, Able and Baker travelled in separate capsules, located in the rocket's nose cone.

During the flight, Able was trained to press a telegraph key in response to a blinking light. This let scientists study her reaction time during the space-flight.

Researchers chose primates for their ability to do a specific job. Able's ability to press a button when lights came on while in space proved that humans could perform tasks in space, too.

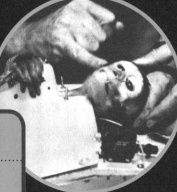

US Army: Able and Baker

Date: May 28, 1959
Species: 3.18 kg (7 lb) rhesus monkey and 0.31 kg (11 oz) squirrel monkey
Objective: Test responses to spaceflight and reaction times during flight compared to reaction times on the ground
Launch Vehicle: Jupiter AM 18 IRBM
Maximum Altitude: 483 km (300 mi)
Principal Investigator: US Army

Custom made

Monkey space suits, helmets, and couches were custom made for each animal.

Miss Baker with her Certificate of Merit from the American Society for the Prevention of Cruelty to Animals.

"To Baker, because this one-pound squirrel monkey, along with her simian companion Able, was one of two American pioneers to travel 300 miles into outer space, thus blazing the trail for human beings who will follow and widening the horizons of scientific knowledge, which will eventually benefit all of us who dwell on the earth, whether animals or humans." — American Society for the Prevention of Cruelty to Animals

"These monkeys are almost volunteers. During the pre-flight testing, we didn't force a monkey to take a test if it objected to it." — Navy Captain Ashton Graybiel

Baker is shown here with a model of the Jupiter rocket. Baker was chosen for her intelligent and docile nature.

07 Two Dogs and a Rabbit

One of the last Soviet suborbital flights carried a rabbit, named Marfusha, along with two canine cosmonauts, Otyazhnaya (a dog who flew 5 times into space) and Snezhinka.

After her successful flight into space, Marfusha produced a litter of baby rabbits, proving that spaceflight did not cause infertility (at least not in rabbits anyway).*

Images of the dogs as "brave" before flight and "relaxed" after flight dominated the Soviet media at this time. It was most likely an attempt to promote "loyalty and devotion," two things the communist government valued in its citizens.

Last Suborbital Dog Flight

Date: July 2, 1959
Species: Dogs and rabbit
Launch Vehicle: R-2A rocket
Maximum Altitude: 212 km (132 mi)
Principal Investigator: USSR

08 Sam, the Rhesus Monkey

A monkey named Sam (after the School of Aviation Medicine) was chosen for an extremely important mission — to test the Mercury capsule that would soon fly the first Americans to space.

Alan Shepard, the first American in space, and Virgil (Gus) Grissom, the second American in space, were there to watch Sam's flight.

Added precautions were put in place to prevent losing Sam when the capsule returned to Earth, including six support aircraft and four ships. The capsule contained two homing beacons and released green fluorescent dye in the water upon splash down.

The extra precautions paid off and Sam was recovered in good shape. Sam did not perform his tests (pulling a lever when a light blinked) as well during his flight as he had on the ground but the space capsule had proven itself safe for human flight.

Size matters

Rhesus monkeys were chosen over chimpanzees for their smaller size and weight.

School of Aviation Medicine

Date: December 4, 1959
Species: Rhesus monkey
Objective: Create and prove airtight capsule with safety restraints and life support
Launch Vehicle: Little Joe Rocket
Maximum Altitude: 85 km (53 mi), 3 minutes of weightlessness

09 Miss Sam

A monkey named Miss Sam was chosen for another important test of the Mercury capsule — the spacecraft that would take the first Americans into space. This test was to confirm the performance of escape systems. Miss Sam was trained to pull a lever during her flight to confirm that it was possible to perform the required tasks during the flight.

Everything was good until Miss Sam's capsule was blasted free from the rocket causing more thrust and noise than anticipated. She shrieked in protest, but before long she calmed down and returned to lever pulling. Miss Sam was safely recovered after splash down.

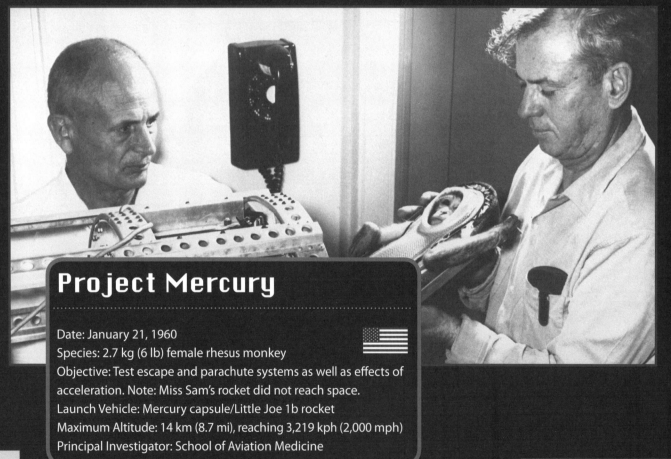

Project Mercury

Date: January 21, 1960
Species: 2.7 kg (6 lb) female rhesus monkey
Objective: Test escape and parachute systems as well as effects of acceleration. Note: Miss Sam's rocket did not reach space.
Launch Vehicle: Mercury capsule/Little Joe 1b rocket
Maximum Altitude: 14 km (8.7 mi), reaching 3,219 kph (2,000 mph)
Principal Investigator: School of Aviation Medicine

Little Joe Rocket

Miss Sam rode in a (simulated) Mercury capsule on top of a Little Joe rocket. These rockets were used because they were much smaller and less expensive than the boosters that would carry humans into space.

The tests showed that the Mercury capsule could be ejected from the rocket and proved that an astronaut could safely be removed from a faulty rocket.

Recovery

While most capsules had been fished from the sea by ships, Miss Sam was the first to be retrieved by helicopter.

Helicopter recovery of a Mercury capsule. (The image shows Alan Shepard's recovery.)

Little Joe rockets were intentionally launched at an angle, pointing the vehicle down range.

10 Belka and Strelka's Safe Return

By 1960 the Soviet Union was almost ready for manned space flight. One of their final tests was to perfect the landing systems of their spacecraft. Two dogs, named Belka and Strelka, were chosen to fly this very special mission. It was the first mission to use cameras to observe the dogs during the flight.

At first it was a stressful flight for the dogs, and Belka got sick (and threw up) just like many astronauts still do today when they first arrive in space. But soon the dogs calmed down, and after 25 hours in space (and about 19 trips around the Earth) Belka and Strelka returned home.

Orbit and Return

Date: August 19, 1960
Species: Dog
Objective: Safely reach and return dogs from space in preparation for manned space flight. Develop Vostok capsule and successful life-support system
Launch Vehicle: Korbal-Sputnik 2
Maximum Altitude: Earth orbit

Belka and Strelka commemorative stamp.

Satellite Dogs

Satellite dogs were those that completed at least one orbit of Earth, as opposed to rocketing skyward and returning immediately to the ground.

Belka and Strelka were the first living passengers to be returned from orbital flight. The mission proved both that the Vostok capsule's life-support system worked and that living things could adapt to long periods of weightlessness.

"They began to run about and jumped high in the air and were visibly pleased to be back on Earth." — Arvid Pallo of the Recovery Team

Love and war

In November 1960, Strelka had puppies. One of them, Pushinka (Fluffy), was given to US First Lady Jacqueline Kennedy. Since this was still during the Cold War, Pushinka was examined by security before being accepted.

Belka and Strelka in the space capsule.

11 Sally, Amy, and Moe

Hair colour

Black mice were used because cosmic radiation was known to turn black hairs grey.

Three Black Mice

Date: October 13, 1960
Species: Black C-57 mice
Objective: Test GE re-entry vehicle RVX-2A
Launch Vehicle: Atlas-D rocket
Maximum Altitude: 1,046 km (650 mi), acceleration to around 27,359 KPH (17,000 MPH), 10 mins of weightlessness

Three black mice named Sally, Amy, and Moe were trained at the School of Aviation Medicine (hence the names). During their flight, minor changes in pulse and breath were noted for only a moment after lift-off. The three mice were safely recovered and showed no grey hairs from radiation exposure.

The mice were launched into space in the nose cone of an Atlas-D rocket. The rocket launched from Florida, at the Cape Canaveral Air Force Station. The capsule containing the mice was retrieved, on target, 8,000 km (4,971 miles) downrange near Ascension Island in the South Atlantic. This flight's primary mission was to test the reentry vehicle, the part of the rocket that would survive the journey back into the Earth's atmosphere. A later version of this rocket would be used to send astronaut John Glenn into orbit in 1962.

Sally and Amy were later mated with Moe to study effects of space-flight on reproduction.

12 The Amazing Rescue

Two dogs, named Zhulka and Shutka, flew shortly after Belka and Strelka on a similar mission to test life-support systems and re-entry from orbit on the Vostok 1K **prototype** spacecraft. Everything was going as expected until their rocket malfunctioned, triggering the emergency separation of the dogs' space capsule from the rocket, before ever reaching orbit. Flight controllers thought the spacecraft was lost until they received a signal from its tracking beacon! Zhulka and Shutka had landed near the Tunguska meteor impact site in Siberia.

The mission was a top secret military project and the spacecraft had a self-destruct mechanism that would explode if the capsule wasn't retrieved in 60 hours. A rescue team rushed to the site and rescuers jumped from a hovering helicopter into waist-deep snow in -45 degree weather.

Frost covered the spacecraft's window, so the rescuers couldn't see the dogs inside. There was no response to their knocking and rescuers feared the worst. They needed to deactivate the self-destruct mechanism if there was to be any chance of saving the two dogs.

The sun sank as they worked and temperatures continued to drop. Finally, the rescuers successfully deactivated the explosives, but it had grown too dark and too cold for them to stay. They would have to come back for the dogs in the morning.

Despite their ordeal, Zhulka and Shutka were recovered alive and well!

The Amazing Rescue

Date: December 22, 1960
Species: Dogs
Objective: Life support & recovery test
Launch Vehicle: Vostok-K rocket
Maximum Altitude: Failed to reach orbit

13 Ham, the Chimpanzee

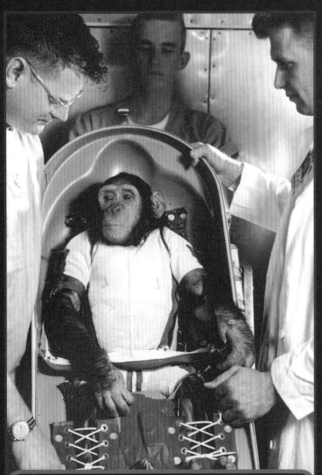

The Mercury-Redstone 2 mission was the second last spaceflight before the first American in space. A chimpanzee named Ham was chosen for the flight for his excellent temperament and alertness. During his flight, Ham was required to pull levers when an indicator light came on. This would show that a human could perform tasks when put in the same situation.

A problem with the fuel mix caused the rocket to accelerate faster and burn out sooner than planned. Ham experienced vastly more acceleration than had been anticipated and ceased pulling levers for a minute until he reached weightlessness.

Despite the challenges and additional **g force**, Ham performed well — proving that an astronaut would be able to carry out required tasks.

Ham also had a rough splash down, but the homing beacon, green dye, and high-intensity light guided his recovery team.

Mercury-Redstone 2

Date: January 31, 1961
Species: 3-yr-old, 16.8 kg (37 lb) chimpanzee
Objective: Precursor to Alan Shepard's suborbital flight
Launch Vehicle: Mercury-Redstone/MR-2
Maximum Altitude: 249 km (154.7 mi)

How Ham got his name

Ham (Holloman Aerospace Medical) was also the nickname of the lab director at the time (Lt. Col. Hamilton Blackshear).

A Bumpy Ride

Unfortunately, the lower heat shield had snapped back so hard that it broke the hull and water started to pour in to Ham's capsule. A malfunction in the relief valve meant the water had nowhere to go. Ham's capsule took on 360 kg (800 lb) of water but was successfully fished out of the sea.

The chimp was a little wobbly and dehydrated with a small bump on his nose but otherwise in good health. However, his good temperament was lost at sea. At the press conference following his recovery, Ham screamed and showed his teeth to reporters and refused to go anywhere near the Mercury capsule for photos.

Mercury capsule.

Alan Shepard.

Heaviest animal

At 16.8 kg (37 lb), Ham was the heaviest animal to be sent on an experimental space flight.

Chimp training school

Ham and Enos (page 34–35) went to chimp astronaut training at Holloman Air Force Base in New Mexico. Here, the chimps learned to sit in chairs and wear special jackets for progressively longer periods of time and a device to test their reflexes was added. The chimpanzees were used to test life-support systems and prove that astronauts would be able to perform tasks during flight. The chimps' task involved pulling three levers in response to three flashing lights. This task would be performed throughout the flight in order to assess their ability to perform under all flight circumstances.

14 Hector, the Space Rat

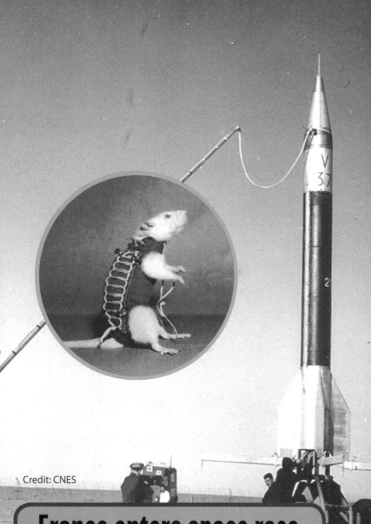

Credit: CNES

France enters space race

With Hector's flight, France became the third country to send a living creature into space.

This experiment was carried out in 1961 by a French organization called "Comit d'Action Scientifique de Defense Nationale" or CASDN. They used a sounding rocket called Veronique, a name derived from the word "victory."

Remember, sounding rockets go high enough to enter space, but not fast enough to maintain an orbit, so they fall right back to Earth. The rocket carrying France's first space rat was launched from a test site in Algeria, North Africa. The rat was safely recovered in good health and after his flight, the French media gave him the name, Hector.

Veronique Rocket

Date: February 22, 1961
Species: Rat
Objective: Study the **vestibular nerve** in zero g
Launch Vehicle: Veronique AG124
Maximum Altitude: 111 km (69 mi)
Principal Investigator: Comit d'Action Scientifique de Defense Nationale , France

15 A Mannequin and His Dog

A dog named Chernushka flew in a Vostok-3KA spacecraft with a very special passenger, a mannequin (a life-like dummy) nicknamed Ivan Ivanovich. During the flight, Ivan was ejected from the vehicle, while the dog remained on board.
Both the dog and Ivan the mannequin were recovered safely.

This spaceflight also included 40 black and 40 white mice, guinea pigs, and reptiles. The flight was a success, bringing the Soviets one step closer to sending a **cosmonaut** to space.

9-III-1961

Ivan Ivanovich
(a dummy).

First watch in space

Upon the dog's recovery from the space capsule, a wrist watch was found on one of her legs. The watch belonged to Dr. Abram Genin of the Institute of Aviation and Space Medicine. He had been trying to get rid of the watch so he put it on the dog. Dr. Genin was severely reprimanded for the stunt, but when he gave an interview about it in 1989 he was still wearing the first watch in space.

Ivan and Chernushka

Date: March 9, 1961
Species: Dog
Objective: One orbit with Ivan Ivanovich
Launch Vehicle: Sputnik 9
Maximum Altitude: Earth orbit

16 Little Star

A dog named Zvezdochka (Little Star) accompanied the life-like dummy, Ivan Ivanovich, on the mannequin's second orbital flight.

All six of the Soviet cosmonauts-in-training were there to watch Zvezdochka's flight, since it would the last test flight before Yuri Gagarin's historic flight. It followed the route planned for the first manned flight.

Except for a snowstorm delaying the space capsule's recovery, the flight was a complete success. The Soviet Union was ready to send the first human into space.

Vostok programme

Date: March 25, 1961
Species: Dog
Objective: Final preparations for Yuri Gagarin's flight
Launch Vehicle: Vostok-3KA No. 2
Korbal-Sputnik 5
Maximum Altitude: Earth orbit

Stamp featuring Zvezdochka

The End of an Era

While Zvezdochka was not the last canine cosmonaut, the dog program came to a close with her flight. The canine cosmonauts had proven spaceflight was possible and opened this new frontier to humans.

Yuri Gagarin: Zvezdochka's flight made Yuri's flight possible.

Zvezdochka was the last dog to fly before humans flew to space.

Staying grounded

Many dogs kept at the Soviet facilities never rode a rocket. These "technical" dogs were still very important in their contributions to related technologies and training.

17 The First Chimp to Orbit

Enos.

Mercury capsule.

Atlas D rocket.

After Ham (page 28–29) another all-star chimp was chosen to fly a test flight in preparation for the first American into orbit. This chimp was named Enos, which means "man" in Greek. Enos received 1,263 hours of training and along with other potential candidates was taken up in a T-38 Talon Fighter Jet trainer to acclimate him to take-off acceleration and the noise of high-speed flight.

Enos had an even more complex instrument panel than Ham, with lights, levers, and symbols. During his mission, there was an overheating problem with Enos's spacesuit (the same problem astronauts later complained about).

The first orbit around the Earth was uneventful, but on the second the spacecraft began tumbling because of a thruster failure. Also, a malfunction caused Enos to receive small reminder shocks even when he performed his tasks correctly.

Despite the thruster failure, the space capsule returned to Earth, and Enos was recovered in good health. Unlike Ham, Enos was very well behaved for his press conference.

Project Mercury

Date: November 29, 1961
Species: 4-yr-old, 17.7 kg (39 lb) chimpanzee
Objective: Precursor to John Glenn's orbital flight
Launch Vehicle: Mercury Atlas 5 Rocket
Maximum Altitude: 2 Earth Orbits, 181 minutes of weightlessness
Principal Investigator: NASA

The Maverick Chimp

Unlike most of the animals on previous spaceflights, Enos was a handful. He didn't take to being held and he was poorly behaved toward guests (even throwing feces at a politician that pulled strings to see him). While Enos had behavioural issues, he was a hotshot and good at his job.

T-38 Talon.

Electric tap-tap reminders

To remind the chimps of their tasks, engineers fitted them with small **electrodes**. These emitted a tiny electric shock. If you have, or have tried on, an Apple watch you have probably experienced the same type of shock that space monkeys would have received. What feels like a tap on the back of your wrist when you get an alert is actually a small and harmless electric shock.

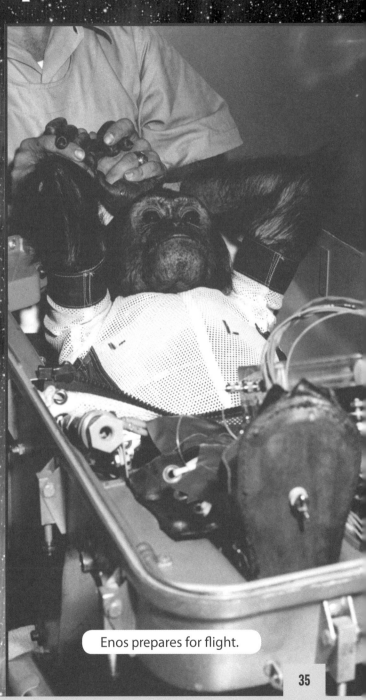

Enos prepares for flight.

18 First Cat in Space

In 1963, an unnamed female stray cat with tuxedo colouring was chosen to fly in France's Veronique rocket as part of a research program sponsored by the French government.

Electrodes were implanted in her brain to record detailed data. Reaching a record height of 156 km (96.9 mi), she became not only the first cat in space but also the first cat to experience weightlessness.

Following her flight and descent via parachute, her space capsule landed safely and she was soon recovered. Only then was the cat given a name: Felicette.

First Cat in Space

Date: October 18, 1963
Species: Cat
Objective: Biological research
Launch Vehicle: Veronique AG147
Maximum Altitude: 156 km (96.9 mi)
Principal Investigator: CNES

Herding Cats

Felicette was one of 14 stray cats from the streets of Paris who were candidates for the rocket flight. She was chosen for her tolerance to stress, and for her size — many of the other cats were too large for the space carriers.

As part of her training, Felicette, and the other strays, spent time getting used to loud noises and the feeling of a **compression chamber**, as well as experiencing **g force** in a **centrifuge**.

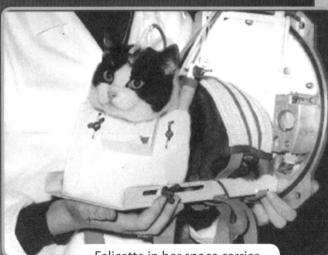

Felicette in her space carrier.

Veronique AG147 rocket.

19 Three Weeks in Space

In 1966, Veterok and Ugolyok became the first canine cosmonauts to ride a Soyuz rocket, a rocket still in use today. The dogs spent a record 22 days in space, helping researchers understand the impact of long duration spaceflight and test the effectiveness of anti-radiation medicine.

The dogs returned in poor health, suffering the effects of the extended weightlessness and restraint. Not only were they dehydrated, they had lost weight and muscle mass, and had weakened **circulation**. This information helped scientists understand the challenges that human cosmonauts would encounter.

It took around ten days for the dogs' motor functions to return to normal. Human astronauts face similar challenges when they return to Earth.

Long Duration Flight

Date: February 22, 1966
Species: Dog
Objective: Testing effects of high radiation in the Van Allen radiation belt and effectiveness of anti-radiation medicine
Launch Vehicle: Soyuz-Cosmos 110
Maximum Altitude: Highly elliptical orbit reaching 901 km (559.9 mi)

Van Allen radiation belt

A zone of fast-moving particles held in place by the Earth's magnetic field.

Veterok and Ugolyok.

The Legacy of the Canine Cosmonauts

The Soviet canine program lasted ten years. Nearly 50 dogs were sent on orbital and suborbital flights, 18 of which lost their lives. Their work was essential in establishing what changes occur to the body during launch, weightlessness, and re-entry. As a result of the data collected on these flights, scientists were able to create the necessary medical and life-support systems for manned spaceflight.

Stamp depicting Veterok and Ugolyok.

Soyuz rocket.

20 French Pig-tailed Monkey

Martine with implanted electrodes.

In the late 1960s, France upgraded to new and more powerful rockets. These new rockets could carry larger **payloads**, and larger passengers. A female pig-tailed monkey named Martine would become the first French monkey in space.

Pig-tailed monkeys were selected because they are compact and docile. Martine performed well, pulling five different levers in a sequence, just as she had been trained.

Martine was successfully recovered. The re-entry capsule's cooling system had not worked as effectively as it was supposed to but Martine showed no ill effects.

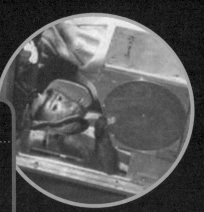

French Space Monkey

Date: March 7, 1967
Species: Pig-tailed monkey
Objective: Test consciousness and motor precision while weightless
Launch Vehicle: Vesta 04 rocket
Maximum Altitude: 228 km (142 mi), 10 g's during ascent

CHAPTER 3
Race to the Moon

American Saturn V rocket.

Soviet N-1 rocket.

21 Tortoises to the Moon

As the Soviet scientists prepared to send humans to the Moon, they designed a special mission to send tortoises first! Two Steppe tortoises were placed in the Zond 5 spacecraft and launched to the Moon, around 384,000 km (238,600 mi) away.

They didn't land on the Moon or even enter the Moon's orbit. The tortoises's space capsule followed a **trajectory** around the Moon that would slingshot them right back to Earth.

The experiments were designed to study the changes in the animals' heath before, during, and after the flight. Zond 5 was recovered near the coast of Madagascar. After being transported back to Moscow, it was finally opened. The tortoises had lost 10 per cent of their body weight but were otherwise healthy. They were the first creatures to fly around the Moon.

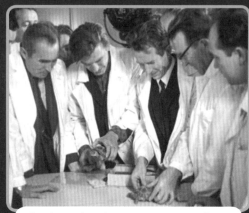

Soviet scientists prepare tortoises for their flight to the Moon.

Zond 5 capsule recovered off the coast of Madagascar.

Stamp commemorating the Zond 5 Moon mission.

Moon Mission

Date: September 14, 1968
Species: Steppe tortoises
Objective: Study chemical changes in cellular and subcellular tissue
Launch Vehicle: Zond 5
Destination: Slingshot around the Moon

22 Fe, Fi, Fo, Fum, and Phooey

Not many people know that five pocket mice travelled to the Moon on Apollo 17. The mice stayed in the command module, and never went down to the Moon's surface. Originally, the mice were identified only by a number, but astronauts renamed them Fe, Fi, Fo, Fum, and Phooey. While the capsule had enough compartments for six mice, only five were flown to ensure that they had a sufficient oxygen supply.

These five pocket mice were part of the Biological Cosmic Ray Experiment. The experiment required no astronaut intervention, but when the pocket mice returned one of the astronauts had left a message on their capsule saying, "For what it's worth, I think I hear scratching on the inside." It was determined that the Apollo command module was so well shielded from radiation it actually impeded the test.

Mouse compartment.

Apollo 17

Date: December 1, 1972
Species: Little pocket mice
Objective: Testing if exposure to cosmic rays caused micro-lesions during lunar flight
Launch Vehicle: Apollo 17 command module
Mission Duration: 12 days
Destination: Lunar orbit

Little pocket mouse.

Every NASA mission has a commemorative patch. This is the mission patch from Apollo 17.

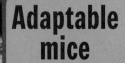

Adaptable mice — Pocket mice were chosen because they are small (7–12 g/0.25 oz–0.42 oz), lower their **metabolic rate** significantly when inactive, and do not require drinking water because they get enough from their food.

CHAPTER 4
Skylab and Kosmos

This Bion/Kosmos spacecraft was uncrewed, but carried many types of animals into space.

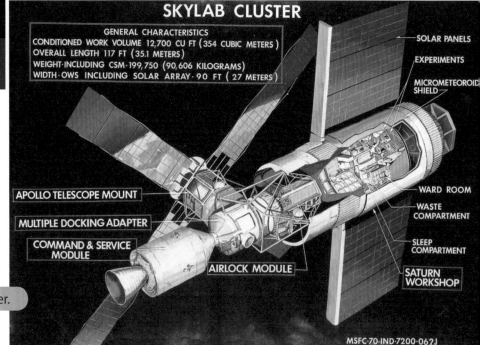

SKYLAB CLUSTER

GENERAL CHARACTERISTICS
CONDITIONED WORK VOLUME 12,700 CU FT (354 CUBIC METERS)
OVERALL LENGTH 117 FT (35.1 METERS)
WEIGHT·INCLUDING CSM·199,750 (90,606 KILOGRAMS)
WIDTH·OWS INCLUDING SOLAR ARRAY· 90 FT (27 METERS)

SOLAR PANELS
EXPERIMENTS
MICROMETEOROID SHIELD
WARD ROOM
WASTE COMPARTMENT
SLEEP COMPARTMENT
SATURN WORKSHOP
AIRLOCK MODULE
COMMAND & SERVICE MODULE
MULTIPLE DOCKING ADAPTER
APOLLO TELESCOPE MOUNT

MSFC-70-IND-7200-062J

Skylab Cluster.

Skylab Student Project

The Skylab Student Project was a joint effort between NASA and the National Science Teachers Association. It was a nationwide contest for students in grades 7 to 12. Over 4,000 students submitted experiments and twenty-five winners were chosen to have their experiments fly to the Skylab space station.

In his report on the project, the Skylab Student Project Manager Henry B. Floyd said, "The simple premise developed that by directly involving students in secondary schools through the nation in Skylab research, these most imaginative, uninhibited, enthusiastic, and promising of all users of knowledge could become intimately aware and personally involved in gaining and applying the new knowledge."

A brief summary of statistics follows:

    National Winners - 25
    Age Range - 14-18
    Mean Age - 15.8 years (Female 15.4,
        Male 15.9)
    Median and Modal Age - 16 years
    Males - 80%
    Females - 20%

Breakdown by scientific disciplines:

    Earth Observations - 2
    Astronomy - 6
    Biology:
        Microbiology - 2
        Zoology - 2
        Botany - 3
        Human Physiology - 2
    Physics - 8

Winners represent 17 states. Their geographic dispersion is shown in the map in Figure 1.

A summary of the Skylab Student Project.

Winners of the Skylab Student Project at the Marshall Space Flight Center, in Huntsville, Alabama.

"Perhaps, in addition to stimulating a group of budding scientists and enhancing public involvement, the Skylab Student Project, through its ideas and new approaches, will stimulate improved efficiency and effectiveness of future space programs."
— Henry B. Floyd, Skylab Student Project Manager

23 Space Spiders

A high-school student named Judith Miles wanted to know how spiders would spin their webs in space. Cross spiders were chosen because they can survive up to 3 weeks without food as long as they have plenty of water.

When they reached orbit, the spider named Arabella was released first. She took a considerable amount of time adjusting to weightlessness, making "erratic swimming motions." The next day she made a small web, which she completed the following day.

Space Spiders

Date: July 28, 1973
Species: Cross spiders
Objective: Web formation in micro gravity
Launch Vehicle: Saturn IB rocket to Skylab
Principal Investigator: Judith Miles of Lexington High School, Massachusetts

Arabella on her space web.

Arabella's Web

The first spider web spun in space wasn't as nice as the web spun on Earth. The web was oddly shaped and the strands were thinner. The experiment was reset and the spider made another web. This second web was much better than the first.

The spider named Arabella was returned to her vial and another spider, named Anita, was taken out and spun several other webs. The spiders did not live long enough to make it back to Earth. Despite this, the spiders became minor celebrities back on Earth.

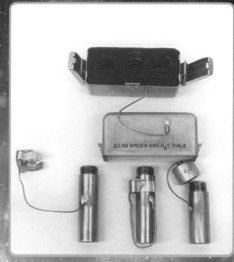
Experiment hardware.

Judith Miles discusses her experiment with Keith Demorest and Henry Floyd of Marshall Space Flight Center.

Preflight efforts

Mr. Floyd's report noted that Judith "experimented with the adaptive qualities of spiders to a slowly rotating environment" even before the experiment took flight.

24 Fish in Space

NASA Researcher John Boyd checks the minnows prior to their flight to Skylab.

Two fish, mummichog minnows, flew to the Skylab space station in 1973. The experiment was designed to determine if fish would become disoriented in zero gravity. The fish were kept in a plastic bag, and fixed to the wall of the space station.

Initially the minnows were disoriented and swam in erratic patterns before visually orienting themselves with the wall they were attached to.

Minnow eggs had been brought along as well. When they hatched, the new minnows had no difficulty in orienting themselves.

Space Fish

Date: July 28, 1973
Species: Mummichog minnows
Objective: Study disorientation in **microgravity**
Launch Vehicle: Saturn IB rocket to Skylab
Principal Investigator: Dr. Garriott

Popular in research

Mummichog minnows are popular research subjects because they are incredibly hardy.

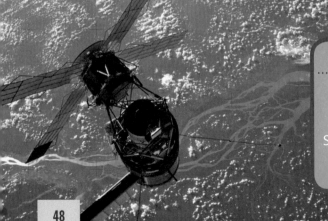

NASA's first

Skylab, launched on May 14, 1973, was the first space station that was launched and operated by NASA. Only three manned missions went to Skylab for a total of 171 days of research. On July 11, 1979, Skylab re-entered Earth's atmosphere and burned up.

25 Rhesus Monkeys

In 1983 a joint US/Soviet mission aimed to study the effect of space on the **cardiovascular system** (lungs, heart, etc.) and **circadian rhythm** (our ability to regulate our sleep cycles based on the day–night cycle). The research would help astronauts on long duration spaceflights, such as today's six-month missions on the International Space Station.

This mission involved two rhesus monkeys named Abrek and Bion, who went through an entire year of training prior to their flight. The two monkeys were placed in a Soyuz-U spacecraft in separate capsules but positioned so they could see each other during the flight.

Two days into the flight Bion's health deteriorated and the monkeys were brought back early. Sadly, Bion died three days later due to a strangled bowel. His death had no apparent connection to his spaceflight.

Abrek and Bion

Date: December 14, 1983
Species: Rhesus monkeys
Objective: Effects on cardiovascular system and circadian rhythm
Launch Vehicle: Soyuz-U Kosmos 1514/Bion 6
Duration: 5 days

CHAPTER 5
Space Shuttle and Mir

Space Shuttle *Atlantis*.

Mir Space Station.

26 Cosmonaut Quails

In 1990 several quail eggs were sent to the Mir Space Station on board a Soviet Progress spacecraft. Once in space, most of the eggs successfully hatched. However, the chicks had significant difficulty feeding in microgravity and required a lot of cosmonaut attention.

Researchers were looking to determine if birds could be bred in space and used as a food source for future astronauts or cosmonauts.

Quail egg **incubator.**

Newly hatched quail.

Mir

Date: February 28, 1990
Species: Japanese quails
Objective: Embryo development in space. Could quail be a space-grown food source?
Launch Vehicle: Soviet Progress spacecraft to Mir Space Station

27 Moths and Flies

NASA's third space shuttle flight (dubbed STS-3) was the first flight to include a project from the Shuttle Student Involvement Project (SSIP) detailed on page 57. STS-3 carried moths and house flies. The experiment involved recording the insects' activities with a video camera in order to determine their ability to navigate and mate in zero gravity. The flies seemed to prefer walking to flying in microgravity but the moths got on just fine.

Flying in Space

Date: March 22, 1982
Species: Flies and moths
Objective: First Shuttle Student Involvement Project
Launch Vehicle: Space Shuttle *Columbia*
Principal Investigator: Todd E. Nelson

Eighteen-year-old high-school senior Todd Nelson describes his experiment.

Moths in their enclosure on the Space Shuttle.

NASA astronaut, C. Gordon Fullerton, checks on the flies and moths.

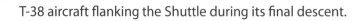

T-38 aircraft flanking the Shuttle during its final descent.

28 Space Bees

In 1984, a colony of 3,400 honeybees flew into orbit. Even the queen bee came along for the ride. This was a student experiment to determine if there would be any differences in the honeycomb made by bees in space. A **control** colony was kept in an identical container on Earth.

Despite being in zero gravity, the bees managed to make their honeycomb. There were some minor differences between the honeycombs constructed in space and those made on Earth. For example, the ones made in space had cells that were angled differently, they were not as wide, and had thicker walls. The queen laid 35 eggs during her time in space, though none hatched upon return to Earth. Researchers couldn't figure out why the eggs didn't hatch. This is still a mystery that requires further study.

Bee enclosure for the experiment.

High-school student Dan Poskevich holds the bee enclosure for his experiment.

Flying in Space

Date: April 6, 1984
Species: Honeybees
Objective: Honeycomb construction in microgravity
Launch Vehicle: *Challenger* STS-41-C
Principal Investigator: Dan Poskevich
Sponsored by: Honeywell Inc.

Quick learners

At the beginning of their spaceflight, the bees would bump into walls when flying but by the end they were very well adapted and no longer had any difficulties navigating in microgavity.

29 Humans and Monkeys Fly Together

Crew of STS-51-B.

Monkey during spaceflight.

One of the monkeys with a model of the shuttle she flew in.

The seventh flight of the Space Shuttle *Challenger* contained a laboratory called Spacelab in its cargo hold. In this laboratory, monkeys and humans worked together in space for the first time. Although the monkeys remained unnamed, they did make friends with the crew. At first, the monkeys stayed in their enclosure, until one of them got sick and the astronauts received permission to intervene. The ailing monkey was handed his banana pellets by a crew member and almost immediately perked up. Throughout the rest of the flight, the monkeys were hand-fed and given a brief period of play with their human crew mates, which was good for their health and happiness. All astronauts, human and monkey, returned safely to Earth.

Spacelab Monkeys

Date: April 29, 1985
Species: Squirrel monkeys and albino rats
Objective: Assess physical and behavioural adaptation to space travel and housing equipment
Launch Vehicle: *Challenger* STS-51-B
Duration: 7 days and 111 Earth orbits

Sleeping Rats

Also on board STS-51-B were several white rats. They gave Pilot Frederick Gregory a fright. When he checked on them they were floating motionlessly and he thought they had died. William Thornton, a mission specialist, told him to tap on the glass. When he did, the rats perked up — they had simply been floating at ease in microgravity.

The astronauts tried squirting water at the rats to see what they would do. The rats simply reached out and brought the water droplets to their mouths as if it were the most natural thing in the world. They learn fast!

Monkeys in Animal Holding Facility during space-flight.

Diagram of Life Sciences Research Animal Holding Facility in Spacelab-3.

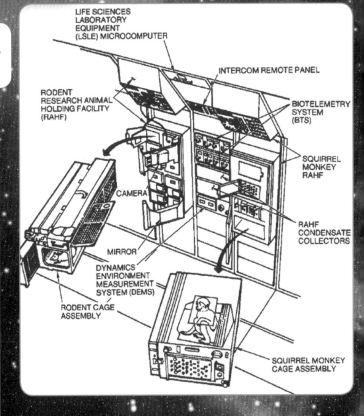

LIFE SCIENCES LABORATORY EQUIPMENT (LSLE) MICROCOMPUTER

INTERCOM REMOTE PANEL

RODENT RESEARCH ANIMAL HOLDING FACILITY (RAHF)

BIOTELEMETRY SYSTEM (BTS)

SQUIRREL MONKEY RAHF

CAMERA

RAHF CONDENSATE COLLECTORS

MIRROR

DYNAMICS ENVIRONMENT MEASUREMENT SYSTEM (DEMS)

RODENT CAGE ASSEMBLY

SQUIRREL MONKEY CAGE ASSEMBLY

"Actually both monkeys adapted surprisingly well to weightlessness, they adapted much more quickly than we did. There is some small difference between the two in the rate of adaptation. Even the rats seem to be moving around quite easily in this totally new environment for them."
— Mission Specialist Thornton

30 Kentucky Space Chicken

A student experiment called "Chix in Space" was created by John Vellinger (a grade 8 student at the time) and sponsored by Kentucky Fried Chicken. Yes, KFC sponsored a student experiment to see how chickens develop in space!

The first attempt of Chix in Space was on board *Challenger* in 1986, but that mission ended in disaster 73 seconds after take-off. Three years later, the experiment was successful on the Space Shuttle *Discovery*. Upon the chicks' return from space, the first chicken to hatch was named Kentucky and donated to the Louisville Zoo.

John Vellinger (left) gives a briefing on his egg incubator.

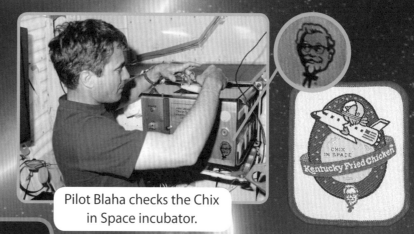

Pilot Blaha checks the Chix in Space incubator.

Chix in Space

Date: March 13, 1989
Species: Chicken
Objective: Determine the effects of space travel on fertilized chicken embryos
Launch Vehicle: Space Shuttle *Discovery* STS-29
Principal Investigator: John Vellinger, Purdue University, IN

Kentucky the space chick.

Scientific Paper available online.

SSIP and the *Challenger* Disaster

The *Challenger* disaster

Several student experiments were on the *Challenger* Shuttle in 1989 when it exploded 73 seconds after take-off. The lives of seven astronauts and all the experiments on board (except hundreds of round worms) were lost. The *Challenger* disaster was a devastating tragedy that put the entire shuttle program on hold until new safety measures were implemented. Because of this break in the program, some students were in college by the time their experiments were flown.

The Shuttle Student Involvement Project (SSIP) was another partnership between NASA and the National Science Teachers' Association. The program was designed to foster student interest in the sciences. It allowed for student experiments to go to space and for students to perform a control of the experiment on the ground.

This program was aimed at students in grades 9 to 12. Twenty-three student experiments were flown between the third and forty-fifth shuttle flights (1982–1992). Students were paired with a NASA consultant and a corporate sponsor.

SSIP participant Amy Kussi meets with astronauts Thomas K. Mattingly II, and Henry W. Hartsfield.

31 Healing Rats

The fifth flight of Space Shuttle *Discovery* included four rats as part of an experiment to understand how healing occurs in space. The science of healing is a very important area of research as humans spend more and more time in space. The rats each had a small piece of bone removed so that researchers could compare how well the healing progressed compared to a control group of rats on Earth. Scientists concluded that the rats in space declined in their ability to heal.

Long-Evans rats

There are many different rat breeds that have been developed in order to study specific health issues. The Long-Evans rats are a multipurpose breed often used to study behaviour and obesity.

Healing Rats

Date: March 13, 1989
Species: Long-Evans rats
Objective: Study the effects of microgravity on healing
Launch Vehicle: *Discovery* STS-29
Duration: 5 days
Principal Investigator: Andrew Fras, Binghamton Central High School, NY

Rat enclosure.

A recipe for success

A student named Andrew Fras (right) was the only student to have two experiments accepted for spaceflight. His other experiment was on the aging of brain cells in space.

STS-29 crew are briefed on Fras's experiment.

32 Tree Frogs in Space

In 1990, six tree frogs travelled to the Mir Space Station on board a Soyuz rocket. Toyohiro Akiyama, the first Japanese citizen and full-time journalist in space, carried out experiments for the Japanese Institute of Space and Astronautical Science.

Japanese tree frogs have small suction cups on their legs. The research concluded that the posture of the frogs in space was the same as the posture they take when jumping to the ground on Earth (all limbs outstretched and abdomen inflated).

When perched in space, the frogs bent their heads back and kept their hind legs partially extended to press their stomachs to the contact surface, not a common position for the frogs on Earth unless they were vomiting. This led to the conclusion that they were experiencing motion sickness.

Tree Frogs

Date: December 1990
Species: Tree frogs
Objective: Test their adaptability to weightlessness and re-adaptation to Earth's gravity
Launch Vehicle: Soyuz TM-11 to the Mir Space Station

Toyohiro Akiyama, the first Japanese citizen in space. Akiyama's passage was paid by Tokyo Broadcasting Service to celebrate the fortieth anniversary of Japan's largest TV company.

33 Moon Jellyfish

The forty-first space shuttle flight was the first space shuttle mission completely devoted to **life science**. Although the Shuttle *Columbia* wasn't capable of travelling to the Moon, it did carry on board a special tank filled with 2,478 moon jellyfish in the polyp stage of their life cycle. It only takes about one week for the jellyfish to develop from a polyp into a fully developed jellyfish.

Many of the developing structures in a jellyfish resemble those in humans. These are relatively simple organisms, making them easy to study, but they still contain a nervous system and an organ called a "statolith," which helps the creatures detect gravity. The polyps developed into free-swimming larvae, which learned to swim normally, despite the weightlessness of space.

However, when the jellyfish raised in space were brought back to Earth, many of them had trouble swimming. This is one of the reasons scientists believe that a human baby, born in space, would have trouble adapting to Earth's gravity.

Space Shuttle *Columbia*.

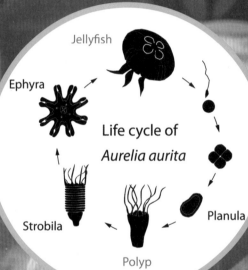

Life cycle of *Aurelia aurita*

Jellyfish

Ephyra

Strobila

Polyp

Planula

Jellyfish life cycle.

Jellyfish tank on the space shuttle.

Moon Jellyfish

Date: June 5, 1991
Species: Moon jellyfish
Objective: Determine how microgravity affects development and swimming behaviour
Launch Vehicle: Space Shuttle *Columbia* STS-40 / SLS-1
Principal Investigator: Dr. Dorothy Spangenberg

34 AstroNewt

Scientific Paper available online.

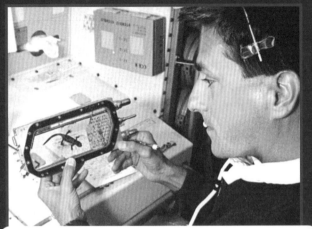

In 1994 the Space Shuttle *Columbia* launched with a complement of fire belly newts. Two Japanese fire belly newts were treated to lay eggs pre-launch and two laid eggs in orbit. Each newt laid about 50 eggs and most hatched. The baby newts were monitored for growth and development to see if there were any changes compared to newts growing up on Earth. There was no noticeable difference other than in their otolith (gravity sensor), which grew twice as large in space.

Astronaut Donald A. Thomas checks on a newt.

AstroNewt

Date: July 8, 1994
Species: Japanese fire belly newts
Objective: Determine whether babies born in space could adapt to Earth's gravity
Launch Vehicle: Space Shuttle *Columbia* STS-65
Principal Investigator: Michael Wiedehold of U of T Health Science Center in San Antonio, TX

Transparency works

Also on board were several medaka fish. Medaka fish were chosen because the fish, egg, and fry (recently hatched fish) are mostly transparent so crew could observe all stages of development. The fish on board the spacecraft didn't show any distress during weightlessness and oriented themselves to a window that simulated daylight. On their third day in space, they successfully mated, becoming the first vertebrates to do so in space. Eight baby medaka fish were born.

35 Crickets in Space

In 1998 scientists sorted through 10,000 crickets to select the 1,514 they wanted to send to space. The group included 824 babies (larvae) and 690 eggs that would hatch in space.

Unlike humans, a cricket's gravity sensors (called interneurons) are located outside their body. With a microscope, it is possible to see how these interneurons develop. A cricket's head movement is also very sensitive to gravity. By analyzing the movement of their heads, researchers were able to determine how the crickets adapted to both microgravity and on their return to Earth's gravity. The crickets were divided into three groups: One was allowed to experience microgravity and the other two were placed in centrifuges at 1G (to simulate one times the Earth's gravity) and 3G. The 1G crickets didn't show any change when they returned to Earth. The microgravity crickets and the 3G crickets, however, had difficulty adjusting and were more sensitive to Earth's gravity.

When asked if the chirping would drive the astronauts crazy, Principal Investigator Eberhard Horn answered that the crickets were too young to chirp. The experiment went so well they repeated it later with female adult crickets. Since only male crickets can chirp, there was no risk that chirping would disturb the astronauts.

Crickets In Space

Date: April 17, 1998
Species: Crickets
Objective: Determine the effects of genetics versus environment on development of sensory, neuronal, and motor systems
Launch Vehicle: Space Shuttle *Columbia* STS-90
Principal Investigator: Eberhard Rudolf Horn

Canadian connection

Students from Ontario designed an experiment as part of the Cubes in Space program to fly crickets on a sounding rocket in June 2018. Their proposal was chosen out of hundreds submitted.

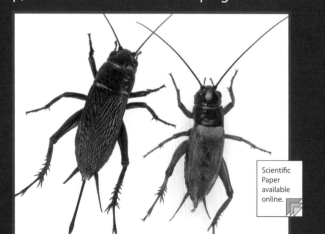

Scientific Paper available online.

36 Oyster Toadfish

Toadfish may look very different from humans but their inner ear is similar to ours. For this reason, toadfish were chosen to help us learn about how microgravity affects our inner ear. The inner ear is responsible for balance. A problem with it can cause dizziness and motion sickness.

The inner ear is tiny but it can affect many other systems in the body, including your vision and digestion. After analyzing data from electrodes in the experimental toadfish, a comparison between the space toadfish and their ground-based counterparts determined that reduced gravity results in increased sensitivity of the inner ear.

The oyster toadfish.

Payload Specialist Chiaki Mukai and Mission Specialist Scott E. Parazynski with the Vestibular Function Experiment Unit that housed the oyster toadfish.

Toadfish

Date: October 29, 1998
Species: Oyster toadfish
Objective: Understand how microgravity affects balance
Launch Vehicle: Space Shuttle *Discovery* STS-95
Duration: 9 days
Principal Investigators: Dr. Stephen Highstein, Washington University School of Medicine

37 Space Beetles

On Earth, when aphids see ladybugs they drop to the ground to avoid being eaten. A group of students from Chile developed an experiment to see if the same thing happens in space.

Four ladybugs — named John, Paul, Ringo, and George after the Beatles — and a horde of aphids rode on Space Shuttle *Columbia*. The results of the experiment showed that microgravity had little to no effect on the ladybugs, but aphids were unable to use their ordinary defense mechanism and were quickly eaten.

Space Beetles

Date: July 23, 1999
Species: Ladybugs and aphids
Objective: Whether an aphid's defense mechanism still works in space
Launch Vehicle: Space Shuttle *Columbia* STS-93
Principal Investigator: A group of students from Liceo No. 1 Javiera Carrera High School, Chile

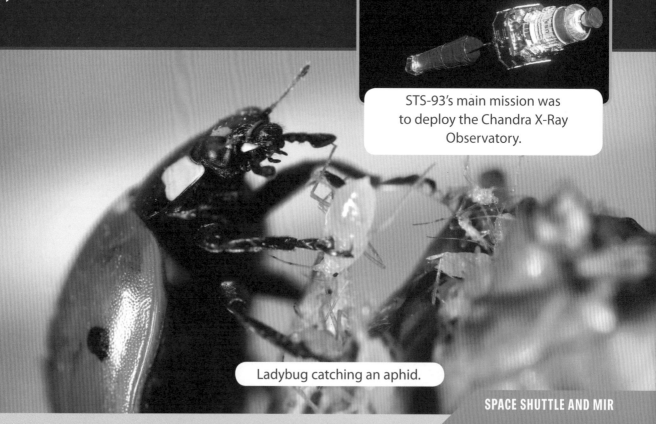

STS-93's main mission was to deploy the Chandra X-Ray Observatory.

Ladybug catching an aphid.

And Butterflies too!

Also on board the same spacecraft was an experiment designed by high-school students from Albany, Georgia. They wanted to know if painted lady butterflies could successfully go through **metamorphosis** in microgravity. The experiment was a success and the butterflies emerged from their chrysalises to be the first of their kind in space.

Eileen Collins

Collins was the commander of this mission and the first female commander of the Space Station.

Painted lady butterflies in their space enclosure.

Ladybugs fly again

This wasn't the only time ladybugs flew in space as part of a student experiment. The students of Mount Carbon Elementary School in Littleton, Colorado, wanted to determine how a ladybug's life cycle would be affected by space travel. These ladybugs flew on top of a SpaceX Falcon 9 rocket to the International Space Station in 2016.

38 Stressed Scorpions

In 2005 an uncrewed spacecraft called Foton, loaded with European experiments, was launched from Kazakhstan on top of a Russian Soyuz rocket. This mission was entirely devoted to biological research, and it contained a variety of living creatures. The animals spent 16 days in space, and returned to Kazakhstan for further study.

Researchers from Germany chose scorpions for this flight due to their hardiness and ability to handle extreme conditions and low food requirements. The goal was to study the scorpion's nervous system and its ability to handle the stress of space travel. In particular, researchers were interested in the animal's biological clock, or circadian rhythm, and the disturbance of it in spaceflight.

Scorpions will fly to space again, this time to the International Space Station. The scorpions will be kept in the European Space Agency's biological research laboratory (called BIOLAB), in the *Columbus* module.

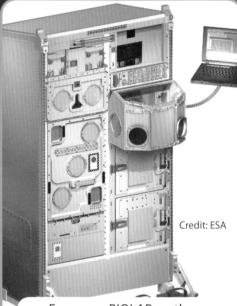

Credit: ESA

European BIOLAB on the International Space Station.

Mission Profile

Date: May 31, 2005
Species: Scorpions
Objective: Study the effects of stress on the nervous system
Spacecraft: Foton-M2 to Space Lab
Duration: 16 days
Principal Investigators: Michael Schmah and Eberhard Horn, University of Ulm, Germany

Scientific Paper available online.

39 Snails in Space

Snails have flown into space three times: once on the Foton-M2 mission in 2005 (along with the scorpions), on Foton-M3 in 2007, and on the Bion-M1 mission in 2013.

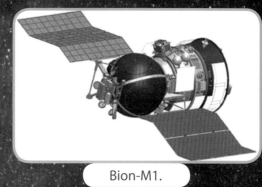

Bion-M1.

Researchers wanted to learn how the animal senses gravity and acceleration. They found many similarities between snails and **vertebrates,** indicating that many of the gravity sensing processes may be the same.

Scientists realized it was important to get the snails back to the laboratory as soon as possible after their return from orbit. After the Foton-M2 flight, the scientists chartered helicopters and airplanes to rush the animals back to the laboratory.

Mission Profile

Date: May 31, 2005, September 14, 2007, April 19, 2013
Species: Snails
Objective: Study sensitivity of balance receptors after spaceflight
Spacecraft: Foton-M2 and Foton-M3, Bion-M1
Duration: 16 days
Principal Investigators: Russian Academy of Sciences/ Space Biosciences Research of NASA

After their return to Earth an experiment was conducted in which the snails were tilted (they prefer to be level) to see if they responded differently than the snails that remained on Earth. They did! The flight snails were more sensitive to the tilt and moved to level themselves sooner than their non-flight counterparts.

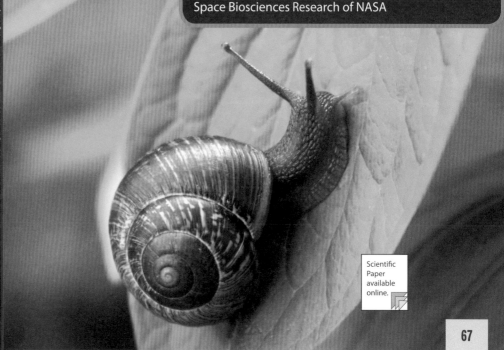

Scientific Paper available online.

40 Tardigrades

Also known as water bears or moss piglets, tardigrades grow to around 0.5 mm long. They are a favourite of those who hope to find life on other planets. Why? These microscopic creatures are known to be able to survive conditions that would kill other forms of life. It is hoped that by studying their incredible resilience we will be able to make advances in radiation protection and even anti-aging treatments.

More recently, the privately funded Israeli *Beresheet* lander crashed on the Moon on April 11, 2019, carrying thousands of tardigrades. They were probably killed but no one knows for sure.

TARDIS

Date: September 14, 2007
Species: Tardigrades
Objective: Learn about radiation protection
Launch Vehicle: Soyuz-U Foton-M3 capsule
Mission Duration: 12 days
Principal Investigator: Swedish and German scientists

A tardigrade viewed through a scanning electron microscope (colour added).

TARDIS

Not the time machine from *Doctor Who* but the name given to this mission: TARDIS (Tardigrades in Space).

Almost Indestructible

Tardigrades are extremely hardy. They can survive the depths of the ocean and the driest deserts. They have also survived all five mass extinction events on planet Earth. For this reason we call them extremophiles — a microscopic organism that lives in the most extreme conditions.

Foton-M3 was a spacecraft developed in a partnership between NASA, Russia, and Montana State University. The spacecraft was designed specifically to take biological samples into orbit.

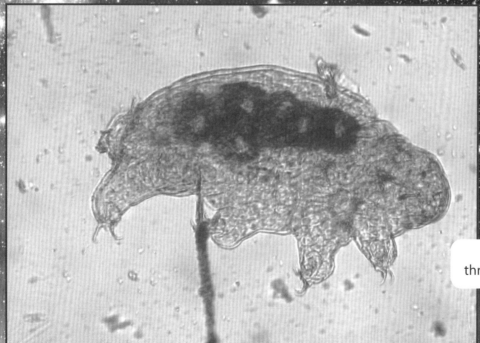

A tardigrade as viewed through a regular microscope.

CHAPTER 6
International Space Station

41 Butterflies

Can caterpillars become butterflies in space? A group of 173,700 students wanted to know the answer. In this experiment, designed by NASA to encourage student involvement in the classroom, caterpillars were kept in a special enclosure and flown to the space station on board the Space Shuttle *Atlantis*. A camera was attached to the enclosure so that students could watch the process from Earth and follow along with their own caterpillar enclosures at home or in the classroom. You can view this experiment for yourself on YouTube.

Monarch butterfly.

Painted lady.

Metamorphosis

Date: October 2008–April 2009;
October 2009–March 2010
Species: Painted lady and monarch butterflies
Objective: Study ability to develop in microgravity
Launch Vehicle: Space Shuttle *Atlantis* STS-129 to ISS
Principal Investigator: Nancy P. Moreno, Baylor College of Medicine, Texas

Air-drying

Monarch wings take 3–6 minutes to dry on Earth but 15 minutes in space.

Space Shuttle *Atlantis* on the launch pad with the caterpillars on board.

42 Space-faring Silkworms

Silkworm eggs were sent to space to see what the effects of cosmic radiation would be on developing silkworms and their offspring. The newly hatched, space-faring silkworms showed no effects from their time in space or exposure to cosmic radiation. The next few generations of the silkworms in space, however, displayed mutations. It is hoped that these studies will help in the development of treatments for radiation exposure and measures to prevent radiation harm.

ESA astronaut Frank De Winne checks on the RadSilk experiment in space.

RadSilk

Date: October 2009–March 2010
Species: Silkworms
Objective: Effects of cosmic radiation and microgravity
Launch Vehicle: Soyuz rocket
Principal Investigator: Toshiharu Furusawa, Kyoto Institute of Technology, Japan

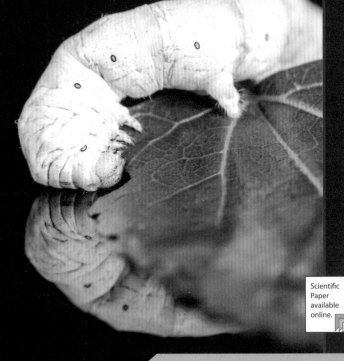

Scientific Paper available online.

43 Space Squid

The final flight of the Space Shuttle *Endeavor* back in 2011 included three baby bobtail squid. The squid had an important job to do. On Earth, luminescent bacteria colonize bobtail squid allowing the squid to become **bioluminescent**. The presence of these bacteria is an essential part of the squids' development. The squid and the bacteria are beneficial to each other (much like **gut microbiota** in humans). The purpose of the experiment was to determine if microgravity would affect the interaction between host and microbe. While three squid is a very small sample size, this study found that the squid and bacteria were able to achieve **symbiosis** in microgravity.

Mission Profile

Date: May 16, 2011
Species: Hawaiian bobtail squid and *Vibrio fischeri* bacteria
Objective: Study the effects of microgravity on beneficial microbes
Launch Vehicle: Space Shuttle *Endeavor* STS-134 to ISS
Principal Investigator: Jamie S. Foster, University of Florida, USA

Baby squid prepared for flight.

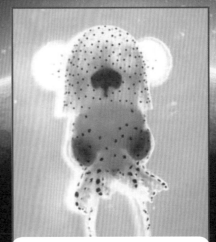

Hawaiian bobtail squid — the first cephalopod in space.

44 Water Fleas

Water fleas are in the crustacean family (just like lobster), but don't grow much larger than a centimetre. They "hop" through the water in the same way that fleas hop onto a household pet. The fleas that flew on this mission were from a lake in Birmingham, England.

Water fleas were sent into space as part of an experiment developed by students in London, England. The experiment looked at water flea reproduction in space and taught students how to establish micro-ecosystems for long-term space flights. The reproductive rates of the creatures were used as a gauge for how much stress they were under during the flight.

Credit: ESA

The experiment was monitored by British astronaut, Major Timothy Peake.

Water fleas are mostly transparent, which makes them easy to study under a microscope.

Water Fleas

Date: April 2015
Species: Water flea
Objective: Study water fleas to improve understanding of how the stressful space environment could impact reproduction
Launch Vehicle: SpaceX Falcon 9 to the ISS
Principal Investigator: Mission Discovery — University of Birmingham and King's College, London

Mission discovery

This experiment was part of Mission Discovery, an international program that enables young students to work with astronauts and create experiments that can travel to space.

45 Ant-stronauts

Scientific Paper available online.

Ants are incredibly good at foraging for food. They are able to search large areas effectively without a central control system to tell them where to go. Understanding the ant's search algorithms might someday improve human search and rescue efforts. By sending ants to space with the ability to change the size of their foraging area, researchers hoped to learn more about their search methods.

The ants were less effective searching their environment in microgravity as they had difficulty maintaining contact with the container. Despite this, they were surprisingly good at regaining contact and returning to their search.

Back on Earth, students set up their own ant experiments identical to the experiment conducted in space (without microgravity, of course) to act as a control.

Ants were held in eight separate habitats. Each habitat was further divided into three sections.

Mission Profile

Date: September 2013–September 2014
Species: Common pavement ants
Objective: Compare behaviour between ants in normal and microgravity conditions and analyze how behaviour is affected by the number of ants in an area
Launch Vehicle: "Ant"ares rocket and Cygnus spacecraft for ISS Expedition 38
Principal Investigator: Deborah M. Gordon, Stanford University, USA

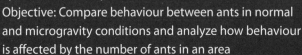

Cameras and computers were used to analyze the movements and interactions of the ants while they were in space.

46 Racing Mice

A group of female mice rode a Dragon to the Space Station — an uncrewed Dragon capsule that is. The space mice were more active than their counterparts on the ground. They developed a behaviour called "race-tracking" where they would run circles in their capsules as if they were racing around a track, apparently using centrifugal force to hold themselves to the walls.

As of 2019, this is just one in an ongoing number of experiments studying rodent behaviour in space. It is interesting to note that the mice quickly develop unique behaviours in microgravity that they couldn't develop in Earth's gravity.

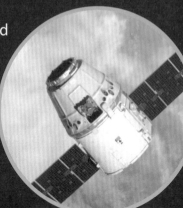

A Dragon capsule.

Mission Profile

Date: September 21, 2014
Species: Mice
Objective: Analysis of adult female mouse group behaviour on the ISS
Launch Vehicle: Uncrewed Dragon capsule to ISS
Duration: 37 days

Mouse Habitats for the ISS.

47 Flight of the Zebrafish

Microgravity is hard on astronauts. While in space, astronauts have to spend hours each day exercising to minimise bone density loss and reduce muscle atrophy. Atsuko Sehara-Fujisawa of Kyoto University wanted to know if the muscles of fish are similarly affected in microgravity.

Zebrafish are a member of the minnow family and are partially transparent, making them ideal test subjects. In space, they orient themselves in relation to light as they would to the sunlight shining down on a lake. Research on these space-flown fish is still ongoing.

Mission Profile

Date: September 27, 2014
Species: Zebrafish
Objective: To learn if microgravity causes muscle changes in fish
Launch Vehicle: Russian Soyuz to ISS
Duration: 1.5 months
Principal Investigator: Atsuko Sehara-Fujisawa, Kyoto University, Japan

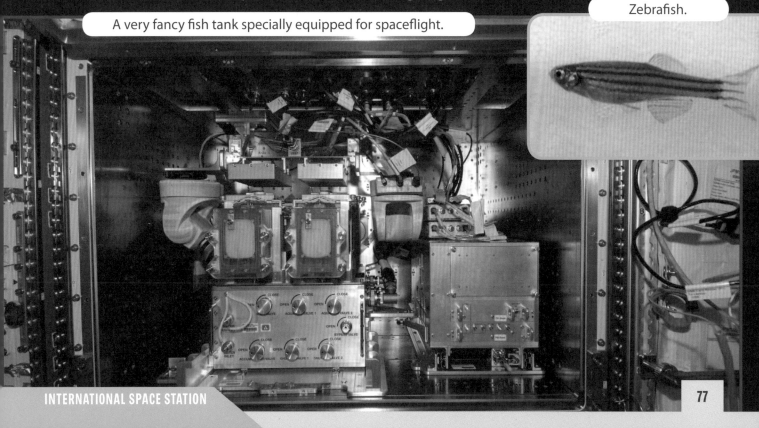

A very fancy fish tank specially equipped for spaceflight.

Zebrafish.

48 Sea-monkeys

Space farming holds promise not only for long-term spaceflight but also as an alternate means of food production for Earth's growing population. Brine shrimp (also known as sea-monkeys) are especially promising because their eggs can be stored without water. Once added to water, the eggs hatch, providing live food for fish or larger crustaceans.

As part of the Student Space Flight Experiments program (which is still around as of 2019) many groups of students in different countries built different experiments to investigate brine shrimp for space farming. The results of these experiments provide useful insight for both **aquaculture** (farming aquatic life) and **aquaponics** (growing aquatic life and plants without soil).

Mission Profile

Date: April 2017
Species: Brine shrimp
Objective: Effects of microgravity on brine shrimp and test usefulness in space farming
Launch Vehicle: Soyuz MS-04 to ISS for expedition 51
Principal Investigators: Valley Christian High School

Sea-monkeys

A popular novelty toy as far back as the 1950s, brine shrimp eggs were packaged in dry form, and then brought to life with the addition of tap water.

49 Sea Stars

Six elementary school students from Pennsylvania wanted to learn more about the vestibular system — the part of the body that helps animals (and humans) keep their balance. They decided to study sea stars because they are very sensitive to their orientation, so much so that they can die if disorientated.

The experiment compared the re-growth rates of sea star legs in space with a control group on Earth. It required the removal of half of the sea star's legs. Because sea stars can shed their legs as a defence mechanism and sea stars have no brain, it is not known whether the process caused the animal any pain. Sadly, the student investigators never got to examine the sea stars upon their return to Earth. The sea stars died, and disintegrated before they were able to get them to a laboratory.

Mission Profile

Date: June 28, 2015 (failure); April 8, 2016 (success!)
Species: Sea star
Objective: Determine if spaceflight presents a balance challenge for starfish thereby preventing them from healing
Launch Vehicle: Falcon 9 Dragon to ISS
Principal Investigators: Aalihya Bowersox and Morgan Schnars of Iroquois Elementary and Junior-Senior High School, Pennsylvania, USA

Unfortunately, the uncrewed Falcon 9 rocket carrying the first sea star experiment exploded just a few minutes after leaving the launch pad. A new group of sea stars flew the following year on the next Space Station resupply mission.

50 Worms Against ALS

Scientific Paper available online.

Annabel Gravely, a grade 10 student from Toronto, was inspired to learn more about **Lou Gehrig's Disease (ALS)**, which claimed her grandfather. She wanted to know if the muscular dystrophy that occurs in space is triggered by the same enzyme that causes muscular dystrophy in ALS patients.

Together with three other students, Gravely designed an experiment using nematode worms. Much to the girls' surprise, the flight worms showed lower levels of the enzyme than non-flight worms. The space worms had also become longer and thicker.

Mission Profile

Date: July 18, 2016
Species: Nematode worms
Objective: Determine if muscle **deterioration** in space is caused in the same way as deterioration due to ALS
Launch Vehicle: Falcon 9 to the ISS
Principal Investigators: Annabel K. Gravely, Alice Vlasov, Amy Freeman, and Kay Wu, Toronto. Dr. Jane Batt, Keenan Research Centre for Biomedical Science of St. Michael's Hospital.

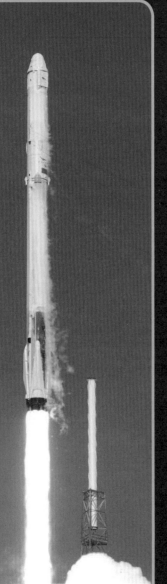

Falcon 9 rocket.

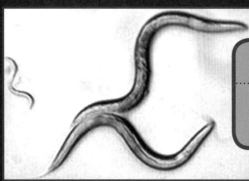

Sole survivors

The nematode worms were the only survivors of the 2003 Space Shuttle *Columbia* disaster.

Canadian Student Connection

"This may be a real finding that could be quite significant for looking at regulation of muscle mass in the future." — Dr. Jane Batt of St. Michael's Hospital, whom the girls approached for help in developing their experiment.

"At any age, you can do science, and you can participate in the scientific process. If you have an idea, don't just kind of ignore it because you think that you're too young to do it." — Amy Freeman, co-principal investigator.

Annabel Gravely and Dr. Jane Batt.

From left to right: Annabel Gravely, Alice Vlasov, and Kay Wu (Amy Freeman not pictured).

Honourable Mentions

Lotte, the axolotl.

During the 1950s most of the rockets used to launch animals into space were German V-2 rockets. However, Germany did not launch animals on rockets until 1961. The first animal launched on German Kumulus rockets was an amphibian called a Mexican axolotl, or walking fish, named Lotte. A second flight, on the same day, contained a goldfish named Max. These rockets were not powerful enough to reach space.

Xiao Bao and Shan Shan.

In July 1966 China sent its first living creatures to space (human missions didn't occur for another 37 years). Two dogs were selected from a group of 30 that had been trained for flight. One was a male named Xiao Bao (Tiny Leopard) and the other a female named Shan Shan (Coral). Each dog flew on their own mission and both Xiao Bao and Shan Shan were recovered in good health.

Kosmos 782.

Despite Cold War hostilities, the US collaborated with the former USSR and sent experiments to space on Soviet satellites. Kosmos 782 (Bion-3), launched in November 1975, was the first Soviet satellite with a US experiment on board. Wistar rats flew together with a centrifuge to determine the effects of micro- and artificial gravity. (Also on board were experiments from France, Hungary, Poland, Romania, and Czechoslovakia.) US experiments continued to fly on Soviet satellites until 1989 and included rats, monkeys, and even fruit flies.

South African three-clawed frogs flew on the Space Shuttle *Endeavor* (STS-47) in September 1992. The frogs were induced to produce eggs to determine if amphibians can develop normally in microgravity. Flight eggs had thicker embryos than Earthbound ones while flight tadpoles had less developed lungs but more developed vision. Also on board the shuttle was the first African-American woman in space, the first Japanese astronaut on a Space Shuttle, and the first married couple to fly at the same time.

Three-clawed frog.

In February 2010, Iran joined the ranks of countries that have sent animals into space. Onboard the Iranian-built rocket was a rat named Helmz 1 as well as several unnamed turtles and worms. Helmz 1 was strapped into a special couch purposely built to hold him securely for his flight. Three years later, Iran sent its first monkey, Fargam, into space and recovered him safely.

Fargam, a Rhesus macaque monkey.

In 2014, ten high-school students from Oregon, USA, designed and built an experiment to send mealworms into space. The experiment examined the life cycle of mealworms in space and if the density of their exoskeleton was effected by spaceflight. Insects are an important part of any ecosystem so it is essential to learn about their ability to survive and thrive in a space environment.

Mealworms.

Mice continue to play a vital role in our medical understanding, both on the ground and in space. A NASA mission called Rodent Research 6 (2017–2018) tested the effectiveness of a medicine that could reduce bone and muscle loss in mice and a drug-releasing implant that could revolutionize how medicines are administered. Researchers are optimistic that this delivery system could be used to combat cancer without side effects.

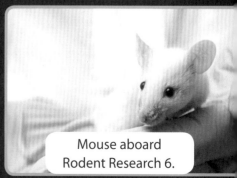

Mouse aboard Rodent Research 6.

Glossary

ALS (LOU GEHRIG'S DISEASE) — A disease that breaks down muscles in the body until the body can no longer function.

ALTITUDE — The height of an object in relation to sea level.

ANESTHETIZED — The process of making something unconscious by using a drug that prevents a person or animal from feeling pain.

AQUACULTURE — Farming in a water environment.

AQUAPONICS — A system where the aquatic plants and animals benefit each other (like in a natural ecosystem).

BIOLUMINESCENCE — Light created by a living organism.

CARDIOVASCULAR SYSTEM — The heart and blood system.

CENTRIFUGE — A rapidly rotating machine that can simulate gravitational forces.

CIRCADIAN RHYTHM — Ability to regulate sleep based on a day-night cycle.

CIRCULATION — Movement in a closed system. Often referring to blood circulation in the body.

COMPRESSION CHAMBER — A chamber in which the atmospheric pressure can be raised or lowered.

CONTROL (GROUP) — Standard to which the experiment is compared.

COSMONAUT — Russian word for astronaut.

DETERIORATE — Becoming worse.

DISSECTION — Studying the internal parts of a deceased creature by cutting it open.

ELECTRODE — A conductor that carries electrical signals.

EXTREMOPHILES — A creature that thrives in extreme conditions that would kill other organisms.

G FORCES — An abbreviation of gravitational forces. This can refer to the force exerted by gravity or acceleration.

GUT MICROBIOTA — Microbes living in the gastrointestinal system that aid in digestion and gut health.

INCUBATOR — Apparatus with a controlled environment to support the development and growth of a young organism.

IRBM — Intermediate Range Ballistic Missile.

KARMAN LINE — The transition between the atmosphere and space. Its accepted height varies between 80–100 km (49.7–62.14 mi) above sea-level.

LIFE SCIENCES — The branches of science that deal with living things.

METABOLIC RATE — The rate of energy consumption in a living thing.

METAMORPHOSIS — The process of changing from one form into another.

MICROGRAVITY — A term used to describe the lack of gravitational pull felt by passengers in an orbiting spacecraft.

ORBIT — The path an object takes around another object.

PAYLOAD — Passengers or cargo on a vehicle.

PROTOTYPE — An early test version of a future product.

RADIATION — Emissions of electromagnetic waves (light or radio) or sub-atomic particles, which in some cases can be harmful to living things.

SOUNDING ROCKET — A rocket used to carry scientific equipment and perform suborbital experiments.

STABILIZATION — Making something more stable.

STATOCYST SYSTEM — The balance system in aquatic creatures.

SUBORBITAL — A trajectory that enters space but re-enters the atmosphere before completing an orbit of Earth.

References

SYMBIOSIS — Mutually beneficial relationship between two organisms.

TELEMETRY — An automated communication process that allows the transmission of measurements made in space.

TRAJECTORY — The path taken by an object in flight.

VAN ALLEN RADIATION BELT — A zone of fast moving particles held in place by Earth's magnetic field.

VENTILATION — Providing fresh air.

VERTEBRATES — Animals with an internal skeletal structure.

VESTIBULAR SYSTEM — A sensory system that provides balance and spatial orientation.

ESA
www.esa.int/ESA

ISS International Lab
www.issnationallab.org

NASA Life Science Data Archive
lsda.jsc.nasa.gov

NASA Image and Video Library
images.nasa.gov

Roscosmos
en.roscosmos.ru/

Science Daily
www.sciencedaily.com

Science Direct
www.sciencedirect.com

SPACE.com
www.space.com

SPACE FACTS
www.spacefacts.de

Spaceflight Now
www.spaceflightnow.com

Research Papers

If you are working on a science fair project, go right to the source! Finding these research papers is easy — simply type the title of the paper (listed below) into a search engine or access the websites shown:

- Student Spaceflight Experiment Program (SSEP) — Information on opportunities for future student experiments in Space. *ssep.ncesse.org/*
- Space Station Research Explorer — *NASA.gov*
- Life Science Data Archive
- Ants in Space — *web.stanford.edu/~dmgordon/ants_in_space.html*
- Avian Embryogenesis in Microgravity Aboard Shuttle STS-29; Effect on Shell Mineral Content and Post-Hatch Performance
- AstroNewt: Early Development of Newt in Space
- Crickets in Space
- Neurophysiological Long-Term Recordings in Space: Experiments SCORPI and SCORPI-T
- The Development of the Hardware for Studying Biological Clock Systems Under Microgravity Conditions, Using Scorpions as Animal Models
- Functional Changes in the Snail Statocyst System Elicited by Microgravity
- Levels of Acid Sphingomyelinase (ASM) in *Caenorhabditis elegans* in Microgravity

- Introduction to the proposed space experiments on board the ISS using the silkworm, *Bombyx mori*.

Many scientific papers are available to read for free online, although you may sometimes need access to a university library. If you are struggling to find an academic paper, you can contact the researcher on *researchgate.net*.

WEBSITES

- *ESA*
- *ISS International Lab*
- *NASA Life Science Data Archive*
- *NASA Image and Video Library*
- *Roscosmos*
- *Science Daily Science Direct*
- *Space.com*
- *Spacefacts.de*

BOOKS

Burgess, Colin and Chris Dubbs. (2007) *Animals in Space: From Research Rockets to the Space Shuttle.* (Springer-Verlag: New York).

Photo Credits

Front cover: Adobe Stock (background)

5: Adobe Stock: top

6: Adobe Stock: top-right inset; India Post, Government of India: centre-right inset; USAF; bottom-right inset

7: USAF: bottom-left; Wikipedia: top-right and centre-right insets; The Met, Purchase, 1871: rightmost inset

8: Adobe stock: top-right; bottom-right

9: Brown University: centre; USAF/NMMSH Archives: right

10: www.nasaspaceflight.com (public domain): centre; Wikipedia: top-right inset; CNES: bottom-right inset

12: circopedia.org (public domain): right

13 Colin Burgess/Robert Sisson: left; White Sands Missile Range Museum: right

15 iStock: background; Asetta / Shutterstock.com: bottom-right

16. British Pathe: left

17. USAF: left

20. forum-conquete-spatiale.fr/ (public domain): left and bottom-right

24. Adobe Stock: centre

25. JFK Library: top-right; Roscosmos.ru: centre-bottom

26. Daily Telegraph, published 16 Oct, 1960 (public domain): left

27. Siberian Times: right-top and right-centre insets; iStock: background

30. CERMA: inset; CNES: left

31. Eric Long, National Air and Space Museum, Smithsonian Institution: centre; Adobe Stock: right

32. Marina P: left; Adobe stock: bottom-right

33. Wikipedia: left; history.nasa.gov (public domain): right

35. US Department of Defense: left

36. CNES: left and bottom-right inset

37. CNES: left; Wikipedia: right

38. Wikimedia Commons

39. Wikipedia: right

40. Dr. G. Chatelier/CERMA: left and right

41. National Reconnaissance Office: right

42. energia.ru: top-right, top-centre; USSR Post: bottom-left

43. Adobe Stock: bottom-left

48. NOAA: centre-right

49. Adobe Stock: right

51. Shutterstock: bottom-left

52. U.S. Department of Defense: bottom-centre

53. Jon Sullivan: centre-right inset

58. Nicole Hönig - Eigenes Bild meiner Frau: top-right inset

59. Masaki Ikeda: top-right inset

60. OIST: centre-right; Adobe Stock: background

61. Adobe Stock: centre-left, bottom-left

62. Adobe Stock: bottom-left

64. Adobe Stock: centre-bottom

65. Smithsonian Institute: left; Jennifer Read: right

66. ESA: top-right; Adobe Stock: bottom-right

67. Adobe Stock: bottom-right, TsSKB-Progress: top-right

68. Adobe Stock

69. ESA: top-right; Gyik Toma: bottom-centre

71. Richie Biits: top-left inset; Tim Bekaert: bottom-left inset;

72. ESA: left; Adobe Stock: right

74. Adobe Stock: background; ESA: top-right

76. Dominic Hart/NASA: 76 (centre); Wikipedia: bottom-right inset

78. Adobe Stock

79. Adobe Stock: centre

80. Ana Gajic, Unity Toronto Health: bottom-centre inset

81. Unity Health Toronto

82. Adobe Stock: top-left; Chinese Academy of Sciences: centre-left; Smithsonian Institute: bottom-left

83. INSA: centre-right (Fargam); Adobe Stock: centre-right (mealworms), bottom-right

NASA images: 5 (bottom), 6 (background image), 10 (centre-right inset), 11, 17 (right), 18, 19, 21, 22, 23, 28, 29, 34, 35 (right), 41 (left), 43 (top-right), 44, 45, 46, 47, 48 (top-left; bottom-left), 50, 51 (top-right), 52 (all 3 insets), 53 (centre-left inset, bottom-centre), 54, 55, 56, 57, 58 (centre, centre-left), 59 (bottom-left inset, background), 60 (top-right, bottom-left), 61 (top-left, centre-right), 63, 64 (centre-right inset), 65 (top-right inset), 70, 71 (right), 73, 75, 76 (top-right), 77, 79 (bottom-right inset), 80 (left), 83 (top-right and inset)

NASA/Bill Ingalls: 39 (left)

NASA/BioServe, University of Colorado: 71 (remaining insets)

NASA/US Army: 4, 10 (centre; centre-right)

All NASA Images follow NASA's guidelines found here: https://www.nasa.gov/multimedia/guidelines/index.html

All flight insignias: NASA

All national insignias: Images in the public domain